Three Days Past Yesterday

A Black Woman's Journey Through Incredibility

Doris I. "Lucki" Allen, Ph.D.
CW3, USA, Ret.

Copyright © 2014 Doris I. Allen

All rights reserved.

ISBN: 1500913146
ISBN-13: 978-1500913144

DEDICATION

To my sister and Commanding Officer,
Jewel L. Allen, Captain, USAR (D)

and to my daughter,
US Navy Lt. Cdr. Hattie M.S. Tapps

ABOUT THE COVER

The Bronze Star Medal is awarded for heroic or meritorious achievement of service, not involving aerial flight in connection with operations against an opposing armed force. The Bronze Star Medal is the fourth highest individual military award and ninth highest by order of precedence in the U.S. military.

A bronze or silver twig of four oak leaves with three acorns on the stem is issued to denote award to second and succeeding awards.

For her service in the U.S. Army during three tours of duty in Vietnam, the author was awarded the Bronze Star Medal. She also received two Oak Leaf Clusters for two subsequent Bronze Star awards.

CONTENTS

	Acknowledgments	vii
	Foreword	x
	Preface	xi
1	Killing People is Wrong	Pg 1
2	Realities	Pg 2
3	I Have Never Been Ordinary	Pg 5
4	A Look In the Mirror	Pg 7
5	Mommie, Mommie	Pg 9
6	You Can't Skip a Beat	Pg 11
7	Welcome Home	Pg 14
8	My Vietnam Conflict	Pg 16
9	Give Up The Ghost	Pg 18
10	Crown Royal	Pg 19
11	Warehouse 5	Pg 21
12	A Man's World	Pg 23
13	The Wailing Wall	Pg 27
14	Help!!	Pg 29
15	I Forgot	Pg 30
16	Just Faces!	Pg 32
17	Anguish	Pg 34
18	I Was Convinced I Was Right	Pg 36

19	The Kiss At The Top Of the Hill	Pg 37
20	Matter of Respect	Pg 40
21	Nothing More to Prove	Pg 44
22	Only When You Die	Pg 45
23	Did You? I'm Just Asking	Pg 46
24	Half-Wrapped	Pg 47
25	You Inside My Body	Pg 48
26	Just Stop	Pg 50
27	Oh Danny Boy	Pg 51
28	Incoming	Pg 52
29	Sisters	Pg 53
30	No Purple Heart	Pg 55
	About The Author	Pg 56

ACKNOWLEDGMENTS

When my unconscious became conscious —only then did I realize that I must write this book. I must thank both my friends and enemies, the naysayers and those with whom I served.

This book is as much dedicated to those who strove to discredit me as well as those who demanded that I write it. It is a product of my educators as well as of my students. I must also thank the men with whom I served. Without them, I could never have grown through the rejection and disrespect which is so a part of the fragile existence as a female soldier in what was so traditionally a male organization. I would like to think that we all grew together as they were able to throw off many of their fears, become the best that they could be and move graciously from "macho" to mature soldiers.

I dedicate this book also to the brave women who served and fought in Afghanistan and Iraq and other countries of the Middle East; they too have suffered against all odds and through much of the same type of disrespect and rejection that was my lot before, during and after Vietnam.

This book is a result of my efforts to escape, albeit unsuccessfully, my pain…the totally undisciplined takeover of my life while I yet live. This book would not exist, however, without the intervention of two accomplished friends, Jovelyn Richards and Elaine Shelly-Burns. Jovelyn, author/actor, put a match to my woodpile and Elaine, author/musician, stoked the fire. Without them, this book would still be scraps of random notes cluttering my living space. Both women encouraged me to "finish" but they did the work—they are my angels.

My sincere thanks are also in order for Rev. Dr. Yvette A. Flunder, presiding Bishop of Refuge Ministries, my spiritual daughter and friend. For more than 20 years, she has guided me through some hard times of anguish, helped me keep the faith in my higher power and fostered my ability to "turn my mourning into dancing."

FOREWORD

I have known Dr. Doris I. "Lucki" Allen for nearly 2 decades as mentor, advisor, confidant, parishioner and friend. After the passing of my Mother in 2007, I came to call her Mom, as she held and continues to hold my heart. We journey together and serve people in our parish and across the world who are among those most marginalized by religion and society. Dr. Lucki's deep caring was molded by the influence of her justice oriented parents and grandparents, and through the crucible of her exemplary military service.

Three Days Past Yesterday is the reflection of a tenacious soul wrestling with the demons and memories of the life and death struggles of fallen and broken comrades who suffered the callousness of those who could have prevented and averted their suffering. These memoirs reflect a series of dichotomies in the soul of a great woman…a fair skinned "colored" woman, a highly decorated woman in a man's world, an integral intelligence officer in conflict with the purpose of a war, the struggle to reconcile loving life and taking life…this is a glimpse of her process as she redirects her fierceness, anger and loss to the continued service of humanity. The absence of a much-deserved hero's welcome for those who endured the obscene loss of sanity, life and limb during the Viet Nam War has left very deep scars on the souls of many of our veterans. It seems that for many, dying would have been preferred to a life of mental anguish, alcohol and drug addiction, the vestiges of Agent Orange, abandonment and PTSD.

Three Days Past Yesterday is a story of hope, told with the raw realities in plain sight. This is the story of a woman who in learning to trust the Divine is teaching other Wounded Warriors from many conflicts, to do the same.

Bishop Yvette A. Flunder
Presiding Bishop of Refuge Ministries

PREFACE

It came to me just now, May 2014, while sitting here in my quietness contemplating my "What's Next?" What became a vivid epiphany: the reason I haven't continued writing my book; the reason I kept lamenting my inability to see the forest for the trees. I finally realized what the trees represented; not that they were obscuring the light at the end of the tunnel so much as they were blocking the entrance.

I know I'm not afraid-I'm not afraid that I haven't (will not have) told my story well. I always knew that the facts were accurate. Since I kept no journal (I eschewed that task) some parts were not detailed but my memory served my recall to validly relate incidents. There was that nebulous block on my self-named "Vietnam-time-brain road" that surfaced so many times as I made attempts to compile the manuscript.

Motivation in so many forms sat on my shoulder. Colleagues and comrades alike were inspiring. Response to questions about my intentions to publish even brought suggestions on methods of publishing as well as avenues to finance the project.
I have been encouraged by published authors and editors. I have had offers of free editing and typing of the manuscript.

Why then haven't I had the audacity to finish the project? The undiluted answer: PTSD! Every time I read one of the stories I am affected by its content. I can't help but relive the moment. I can see the incident that inspired each line. It's the trigger that makes me experience that sad feeling every time I think of a soldier fighting to live or even to die as the case may be. In a piece of my heart there is a screaming, a yearning, a raw impulse to satisfy this anger that supervenes when I think of the ones who sit at poolside and bask in the "shade" of the sun or stand on the green waiting for their turn to yell "Fore" even though they don't give a damn who's listening.

This anger is blatant and comes out when I think of myself getting angry. It is of no consequence that "they" take no responsibility for the decisions that resulted in the deaths of so many. It is of even less consequence that many of "them" are still, more than 40 years later, sitting at the helm and sending even more "volunteers" to their death.

But now!! This present!! I can no longer hide under the cloak that I thought would make me invisible; the one out of which I could not see but realize now that I am really there hiding from ME! Hiding from me!

These stories represent only a smidgen of my intent to NOW tell you the rest of the story.

KILLING PEOPLE IS WRONG

When I left Vietnam, I was determined that I had done all that I could do to win the war, to keep our troops out of harm's way and to keep the faith that so many more of us would not die in vain.

Over the years, my mind changed—my premise changed—my life changed. I was bound and determined then and there to never go back. I would positively never again go to war. I would never go back to the "scene of the crime."

I had a taste of war. I didn't like it. But that taste just lingers; worse than onions and much worse than garlic breath. It's not my imagination! And just when I thought it was just an aberration, along came more death and more killing. I still can't understand why people kill people to show people that killing people is wrong!

REALITIES

First, I want you to know that I did not kill anyone while I was in Vietnam. I did, however, have my own realities.

I saw so many half arms and legs. One vivid memory sort of sticks with me. I remember being in the hospital triage area where the helicopters deposit their human cargo. Triage by the way is where they decide who will get treated first based on so many factors but mainly the severity of the wounds and whether the effort to treat the wound is worth it. In other words, will you live or die if we don't tend to your wounds first. Some were rushed into adjacent areas to be "saved" if humanly possible. The others usually got a shot of morphine or Demerol to await treatment ASAP.

My reality zooms across my consciousness as I again recall the chopper coming in stat with five seriously wounded grunts (GI's - soldiers). As I reached over to move a helmet there on the gurney next to this one bleeding fellow, I noticed there was a ridge inside the helmet - all the way around.

This youngster had been shot and wounded in several places but the shot that hit his helmet spun around inside between the helmet shell and the liner. He was given an injection of Demerol and his gurney pushed aside to wait his turn. I knew then that a higher power reigned over all of us there in Vietnam.

My reality was seeing the women in Saigon in their colorful ao-dais as they walked with pride - as if nothing was going on except the rent, that nothing untoward was happening - as if there was no war. The restaurants were open for business. Doctors walked down the street in their black tunic suits with their white cuffs rolled up. Incense burned to pray for forgiveness and the souls of those gone on.

Fresh food was placed at small altars located everywhere. The black market shops made sure there was no dearth of American cigarettes and Schlitz beer. There was the ever-present ugly American in the person of a drunk soldier shouting unkind words to anyone in his path.

My reality includes watching little children pick through garbage in front of my hotel -- thinking at first that they were looking for bits of food but later learning that they were searching for anything to help defeat their enemy - the ROKs (Koreans) and Thais and Aussies, the ARVN (South Vietnamese) and the Americans.

My reality was watching one of the hootch maids flying a red kite at noon every day. It took a while to figure what she was doing - she was of course signaling and giving information of any and all types to her VietCong comrades outside of the compound.

I so often wondered what saving grace there might have been for the half-price whores who passed on tidbits of information to their VietCong pimps. Lord knows, the enemy had but to read our newspapers to find out all about us - what we would do, when, where and how.

Even now, this quarter of a century later, I still cringe as I hear a helicopter - the sound hasn't changed. My thoughts run back to the wonderment of the flares on little white parachutes - we had to prolong the night to deny the enemy the precious cover of darkness.

My reality is that unlike some others, I can't forget Vietnam and its pain. I tried for a while pushing Vietnam from my mind. Whether out of exhaustion, boredom, disgust or a sense of failure, I just couldn't let go.

I still can't let go. I don't want to let go.

I HAVE NEVER BEEN ORDINARY

From the time of my very first knowing, I knew that I was unique. Mom and Dad saw to that. That knowledge of uniqueness was reinforced every day. My teachers at Douglass High and Grammar School (named for the great Negro educator Frederick Douglass) in El Paso, TX, kept me aware that I was like no other individual on earth. My erstwhile teachers at Tuskegee Institute (now University) founded by another great educator and iconoclast Booker T. Washington, made it perfectly clear that unless I was unique I could never even graduate from that great Negro institution.

Lessons learned at an early age included the ageless adage that knowledge is power. My mother and father echoed a saying that I have found to be esoterically true: Get your education and no one can take it away from you. In that age of Black and White and Colored and restricted water fountains whatever I had earned could be taken from me without so much as an explanation as to why. I surely recall the days of being physically deprived of an earned benefit just because. Mom and Dad made up verbally for what might have become a permanent mental schism as we were denied entrance into certain hotels and movie houses and other places of entertainment just because.

My siblings helped instill my belief that we were rich. At least we were never hungry. I do recall one day, and only once, that Mom had forgotten to give the "maid" some cash for a loaf of bread. Dear Amelia went to the cupboard and found one very old, very stale hunk of bread and broke it in pieces to divide among us. Just before she put it on the table, one of the most terrifying little bugs jumped out. Just before it met its maker, it looked at us as if to say, "Leave my food alone; you don't want us chiggers to have nothing."

I mentioned hunger only in passing because there was always plenty of food for us and our many friends who seemed to always be there. We were taught to hunt and fish from two masters, Mom and Dad, though it was hard getting me on horseback that first time. I was only seven but I knew what the sign "Ride at your own risk" meant. To me, it meant that the other kids would ride off into the sunset and if I got lost no one would find me. Mom, who was standing there, assured me that no matter what risk I took in life that she and Dad would always be there to help guide me. She also said that if I never took a risk that I would never taste life—that there were bad risks and dumb risks and foolish risks and only I would be responsible for my fate.

And only then did I mount the horse—on our next outing and henceforth, I rode Ginger, the most spirited horse in the corral. And so it goes—I have never been ordinary.

A LOOK IN THE MIRROR

Did you ever see a dream walking? Well, I did! I looked in the mirror this morning and saw this gorgeous "older" woman. It was me. I looked at this image and saw myself many years before. I looked so wonderful in my crisp uniform. I can almost hear some of the conversations as I sat on the floor in the barracks with Tuncie and Fran and Connie and Linda. Oh, how we laughed and laughed. Sometimes, we were even soothed by the sound of silence. No, it wasn't due to a lack of things to say, but rather a contentment to be sitting with friends you didn't have to impress.

Back then, we talked so freely about our passions. You see, we all had dreams of freedom. We wondered how it would feel to be allowed to sit in the front of the bus. We opened our hearts to not just each other, but so easily to the sun and stars. And the sky was so clear and beautiful.

And just as quickly as I glimpsed some of the beauty of those days, the wake-up thoughts of having to go back to work in cramped offices with cramped-up officers and NCOs brought me back to stark reality. The possibility of freedom that had permeated my dreams was no longer. I found myself holding onto to this horribly disfigured hand in Vietnam. There was no drama as I tried in vain to shake off the post traumatic stress that had become a part of my life. I dream of flat-bed trucks in convoy being destroyed in ambush and of my friends sitting helplessly as they hear the whistle of the 122mm rocket blazing toward their hut and the cacophony from the ammo dump, the world's largest mass of ammunition in one location and just three blocks from my hootch as it all detonates effectively reducing our own "shoot-back kill them first with bigger shit" capability and me running, running, running so that the Agent Orange designed only to defoliate and make the area less vulnerable to the enemy sapper won't catch me and give me cancer, which has no cure and on and on and on.

But, standing here now looking in my mirror, I feel so insulated from unwanted "people things" around me. And the wonder is that I could forgive myself for being a part of the mayhem. Even now, though it conjures all by and of itself, I can still lose myself in my prayer womb. I can hide from anything and anybody if I feel so inclined.

But today, today, I no longer need to hide cause when I looked in the mirror this morning, I saw this gorgeous "older" woman and it was me.

MOMMIE, MOMMIE

Sometimes, more often than not nowadays, I call out for my mommie. Before, it was always "Mother" when I needed her. I remember back when I was just a young'un when we used to call her "Mama."

One afternoon, she was having a meeting with her societal cronies and after my siblings and I interrupted, unnecessarily several times, my mom asked us to hold on for a few minutes until the meeting was over. She would talk to us afterwards. Mom called us all in and asked if we could call her something besides Mama because she was getting tired of "Mama this and Mama that and Mama this and Mama that." Of course, we four kids were cracking up because she mimicked us with all the gestures included. So naturally, we asked what should we call her. She was still our mama. Her simple reply, "Why don't you just call me Mother?"

But somehow when anything makes me anxious or sad – whenever I'm in mind trouble –whenever I think about soldiers out there thanklessly fighting and dying – when I see the homeless sign-wearing people on the freeway exits and bridge exits – when I read the sad stories about the posthumous awarding of a purple heart to a WWII corporal who lost his leg in France in 1944 – and even when through media-generated information – I find myself reliving some of those tragic moments and feelings and disappointments from my own war zone.

I don't want to feel anymore, but my sleeping hours are all awake because my dreams are of war. I shoot people every night. Almost every night I find myself enjoying the company of friends, then with no warning, I'm surrounded by uniformed warriors. I can't even identify the enemy. All the faces are the same – black and white and brown and yellow and sallow and mean and ugly and grimacing and grinning and even though I shoot them, they never die. Some get up and point their guns at me. They shoot me, but I don't die.

And sometimes something triggers unhappy memories though I never dream of politicians.

I spent ten combat campaigns in Vietnam from 1967 to 1970. I can't go back to Vietnam. I earned three Bronze Stars—no Valor—but after all, what is valor? Valor is what our women and men of today are made of. And I betcha, like me all those years ago, they can't look at a face and boldly proclaim, "That is the face of my enemy."

So when I wake up from my dream—and most times I fight myself awake just to quell the mayhem—I find myself in a struggle to remember the dream. I don't want to forget. I do want to forget. I don't want to forget.

It's all so confusing, especially in my new autumn years. I find myself calling out for "Mommie, Mommie." But now I know Mommie can't help me.

Only God can. Only God can.

YOU CAN'T SKIP A BEAT

As I pondered on patience and attitude and respect and some of the other traits of which leaders are made, it dawned on me that there were other people in my life who helped shape my own character.

I once had a commander during the early years of my military career who embarrassed me to tears in front of an entire battalion of women. On the very day I formally received my promotion to that coveted rank of NCO (Non-Commissioned Officer), I almost lost it.

I was so proud that day. I was so proud not only to have been selected but even more so because my sister was there to witness this next step on the ladder to success. This was the big sister who had cared for me and tended to me while my parents were at work and who helped mold me and by example, groomed me to endure and overcome the vicissitudes of life.

Unfortunately, all did not go well. We troops all fell into formation at 0630 hours, dressed to the nines for formal inspection and to participate in the promotion ceremony. This was traditionally a time of celebration. It was a day that saw so many emotions.

There was sadness in some for not having been selected for promotion even though they were eligible by virtue of being "in the zone." In some, there was envy and jealously, in some downright anger for having been passed over. Yet in others there was pride in seeing their comrades reach another level to which most aspire. In all, however, there was that sense of hope – hope that there was room at the top. For those who outranked the newly promoted, there was a true sense of pride in having been a part of the leadership to make better soldiers of us all. For those promoted, there was happiness, pride, a sense of accomplishment and most of all, a sense of worth.

We, the promoted, each broke ranks as our names were called out and one by one strode smartly to the front of the formation and stood tall. The First Sergeant announced to all, "Ma'am, the troops are all present and accounted for and ready for inspection." This was such a memorable occasion as the words of the Commander boomed out across the tarmac as she signaled approval of the troops and congratulated the five new NCOs.

Her next words, were pivotal and scary to a degree but definitely caused a great positive change in my pursuit of perfection and success as a soldier: they were spoken directly to me. The words were occasioned by my neglect to sew on chevrons of my new rank – all the other newly promoted women had. "Sergeant Allen, or is it still Corporal as indicated by the rank on your uniform?" Looking at her watch, the CO continued her admonishment. "It is exactly Zero Six Thirty Hours – at Zero Seven Hundred Hours, I want to see you in my office with your correct chevrons indicating your present rank on six complete uniforms." And without further adieu, she summoned the First Sergeant and departed the formation in full stride.

Normally, I would have been the proudest troop in the formation. After all, I had just been promoted by the sharpest officer on all of Camp Stoneman (California). Proud not only because she was a Black female officer – there were so few Black female officers anywhere – but because this wonder of a woman was my own sister, 1st Lt Jewel L. Allen.

Actually, my pride was still foremost but as I thought about what had actually happened I realized that on a very personal level, she was also embarrassed. All of her troops were "strac" and ready except for one.

Over the years I found that there was always somewhere that "Except for one." I learned on the fateful day, however, the true meaning of leadership. As my sister stood before that formation performing an act of admonition while at the same moment extending congratulations, it was noteworthy that she hadn't skipped a beat. The fact that her own sister was the "except for one," might have shaken and unnerved many commanders, but it didn't even seem to faze her -- she didn't skip a beat.

During many of the moments when I presented what I considered viable intelligence that was not accepted, I thought of Lt Jewel L. Allen. I recalled that she taught me how to separate the bullwheat from the chaff, how to keep on through the task. She enforced my knowing that oppression led to depression only if I allowed it. The times I wanted to give in were thwarted – through the frustration I knew that I had to keep on task and do the work. And with that armor, even though it took embarrassing tears through my frustration, it was so apparent that, like my favorite commanding officer, skipping a beat would be totally unacceptable.

Through all of the periods of dealing with "Doubting Thomases," it was apparent that it was O.K. to develop a healthy skepticism but unacceptable to let it stop the process. It was just not acceptable to SKIP A BEAT!!!

WELCOME HOME

The blood trickled from my broken heart – not once – not just twice – many times.

The blood trickled as I watched my comrades come home alone –their good buddy left on the end of a punji stick. The trickle persisted throughout my sojourn in Vietnam and even after I returned to what?

And even now it trickles as the strains of that violence-provoking song extolling the rocket's red glare and the bombs bursting in air literally rings out across the nation.

The blood trickled from my broken heart as I stood before a map of South Vietnam and the tears blotted out my vision of the pins and acetate depicting calamity.

And My Lai and Bob Hope and Betty and Frannie smoking pot and every day a fifth of Crown Royal to blot out the pain and less than three minutes away from being splattered all over the Bomb Squad's Quonset hut along with five friends when the 122mm rocket sent them to kingdom come and listening to a full intelligence chain of command from the sergeant to the bird colonel deny that "50,000 Chinese" were on their way to wreak havoc on that most holy of days with their Tet offensive and watching them through my mind's eye as five ammo flat beds were blown to bits and five men were never to be recognized again and 19 could never again be whole and the blood still trickled when I knew the CO wasn't killed in action. He was actually fragged by the Sp5 whose anger at the injustice in the point-guard assignment to all his Black brothers guided his arm in throwing the pinless pineapple into the CO's hut and then

When JFK and MLK were assassinated…

And then when my sisters and brothers sat out in the desert

waiting for mustard gas which never came—but they're still waiting.

And the blood still trickles when I see the flags wave and I know, yes, I know.

That you don't really mean it, America, when you say, "Welcome home!!"

MY VIETNAM CONFLICT

They sat in their ivory tower and maneuvered us like chessmen to annihilation. Being a trained interpreter of conditions and analyst of affairs of the mind and heart, I have tried innumerable times to close the loop. I will never again go to war. I will never forget the war. We lost the war.

I couldn't go to the Wall. I've thought about it. There might have been too many people at the Wall and I'm jealous because all those dead guys belong to me.

Did they cover up wickedness with Christianity or patriotism? Did they start out with a natural propensity for evil? I can only evaluate them from within my realm of experience.

Ugly duckling will even follow a red cloth.

Healthy emotion. When you reach a conclusion, reasoning and thinking stop.

One can only wonder about the pungency of my genius.

> You stole my sons and daughters
>
>> They spent time across the water – fought and died – then came back to cheerless homes.
>
>> No brothers or sisters to greet us.
>
> Just Mother saying, "Welcome home."
>
> Some in the rice swamp – killing shacks and wooden huts
>
>> And we kept raining bullets on villages –

Nobody home – and when I found out I hadn't died, that's when I really cried.

And I still cry –sometimes all night long – cause I still can't figure out if something's really wrong.

Or is it that this thin skin is longing for – nay, yearning for – the touch of the dead?

GIVE UP THE GHOST

I shot at, to kill, so many Viet Cong last night. My guardian brother handed me an M16 and told me to use it when the bad guys showed up. I had a compulsion to kill them only because they were going to kill us. I think that we started out with three or four rifles between us, but before long, there were enough to fight off the Cong.

But they weren't only Cong Vietnamese. They were also some Americans who we figured must have defected back during the war or somehow had moved with their families back to the North.

Now my dilemma has to do with my "killing" all those bad guys. But they never die. They fall down, but they are not dead. In fact, it seems as though they are players who when they die, they're out of the fray, but they never die.

And I get shot, I think, but even I never die. I keep shooting and "killing" them until I am compelled by some blind force to wake up from that horrible dream.

Baffling in a real sense is the fact that this is a recurring dream. I mostly recognize the enemy and I "kill" but he doesn't die. I don't die, but here's the rub, I wonder if he will ever die. Maybe if he is finally dead for good, I can stop killing and the dream will go away. But am I myself prepared to give up the ghost —to die?

CROWN ROYAL

"I can work anywhere—inside my mind or out of it." L.S. Carlin *Out of Darkness*

Sitting "safely" in my bunker, I sipped Crown Royal. All the mortar and rocket noises were safely inside my fatigue jacket pockets. The only weapon in my bunker was my Crown Royal – there were no Clint Eastwoods or John Waynes.

In Vietnam, I became sure that death would last much longer than my life. That meant nothing except what I allowed it to mean. My mind's eye stayed focused – mostly on the rice paddy. Think anything I feel like thinking. Actually "heaven" was forgetting.

Sleep? My eyes itched so often but unlike some of my friends, I didn't mind going to sleep. I knew I wouldn't wake up dead. Some of my friends drugged themselves to prevent their dreams. Most of the time too drugged to be scared and too scared to get tired. Proof of being alive was being able to find your bottle and taking a drink to stave off fear. I was already the "old lady" among my colleagues so I already knew to keep my drinking below the hangover next day level. Between God and my bottle of Crown Royal, I knew I'd make it through each day.

But then came Wednesday – my "health" day. I couldn't have made it without a health day. That was the day I regrouped –the day I cleansed my mind –the day I contemplated the rest of my life. There was no respite from the outrage of this war – no respite from the conflict that had started forming in my mind.

The phrase "war is hell" took on new meaning because now, I was right in the middle of the uncertainty. It was during those health days that I began to know that I was in the wrong place. I began knowing the wrongness of our involvement in Vietnam.

WAREHOUSE 5

Warehouse 5*. I passed it yesterday. TRIGGER! But that wasn't what started it all.

The psychologist asked me some awfully leading questions Monday. You see, I was invited to be part of a research study looking for ways to "treat" my pain. They want to know if one more pill can stop this misery in my brain—this misery that makes me jump, this misery that startles me every time I hear a loud crackle or a balloon pop or sound of a chopper overhead or, or, or…

Then there's that persistent dream so many times when sleep comes—bed time or nap time—I kill people on a battleground, but they never die and they kill me, but I never fall—and I can't or won't identify my foe. And I don't know whether I wake up because of the nightmare or do I fight within myself to wake up and stop the misery. Sometimes, the battle is so vivid that I live it again in my wakefulness—shot for shot and tear for tear. But then sometimes, I feel the misery of the dream with no vision of what occasioned it.

Tears dimmed my eyesight as I answered the researcher's questions about my war that "hurt my feelings" 40 years ago…about that war 40 years ago that taps my brain and causes so much misery.

And people never see the misery inside because I've become a master of disguise. And I'm good. I'm so good that you, you outside my body will never see the chaos or hear my screams or feel the fear that so often wracks my brain.

But when you outside in your innocence dare to see/question my cognitive…

*Warehouse 5 at Oakland Army Base, Oakland, CA, was the morgue where the bodies of U.S. military casualities from Vietnam were held for identification and preparation for future memorials.

A MAN'S WORLD

It's a man's world, but you can't prove that by me. When I was a little girl, I knew that a woman's place was "in the kitchen." That's what I was taught, but I never could understand it because my mom was always away working somewhere. I think Dad spent more time in the kitchen than Mom did. Or so it seemed. Maybe that wasn't the case, but I can remember the first thing my brothers and sisters and I experienced in the mornings was the ride to the kitchen on the shoulders of my dad. In those days, we washed teeth and face and everything else after we ate breakfast. I think that was such a good idea. After all, we were just going to eat some more food and get our teeth dirty all over again. Mom did have a wash cloth at the table so we could wash our hands before eating the food God gave us. Every morning we asked God to "forgive us of our sins and make us worthy of these blessings for Christ's sake. Amen!"

Grandma spent time in the kitchen when Mom and Dad were out working. While she was cooking, I was out playing with the other kids.When it was time for supper, we all had to come in, wash up, all sit down at the dinner table and again ask God to forgive us of our sins.

We always ate in the dining room because it was unthinkable to forego our evening ritual. Dad at the head of the table would begin the evening meal, after prayer, with some news event of the day. Mom added her tidbit. Then came time for the coup de grace. We kids each had to report on an event that we had read in the newspaper that day. Our parents were firm believers that education and discipline should begin at home.

I think I missed some part of my life at that age because I can't think of a thing that went on except that Joe Louis beat the stuffing out of Max Schmelling. I also remember that Jack Johnson was the real fighter who drove fancy cars, wore fancy clothes and drank a lot. There wasn't a lot of that history-in-the-making written in the daily newspapers, but we did receive The Pittsburgh Courier. The Courier was the most read and circulated Negro newspaper in the country. We got the scoop on what the Negro folks were doing all over the United States. Jet and Ebony magazines were still a dream in John Johnson's world.

The Pittsburgh Courier kept us informed about Josephine Baker and Paul Robeson and Katherine Dunham, among others. La Baker made her name in Paris and for many years was denied "diva-ship" in the august halls of America's entertainment world. Paul Robeson's deep bass voice was but a beautiful glory of sounds which he wanted to share with the world but was denied expression on the American stage. He was labeled a communist and therefore, persona non grata in his native country. The phantasmagoric costumery of Katherine Dunham and her colored world-renowned dance troupe made us all anticipate her appearance in our community.

Women who weren't part of the entertainment world were seldom talked about, much less written about in the tabloids of my early days. We knew that Marion Anderson had a wonderful contralto voice which should have been heard at the New York Metropolitan Opera House and at La Scala. We knew that Mary McLeod Bethune founded a university and was a dear friend of Mrs. Eleanor Roosevelt and her husband, Franklin Delano, the president of the United States. Mrs. Bethune was also the catalyst for allowing women to join the military in World War II. Paul Lawrence Dunbar was the poet of our time. We read all about our history in the Pittsburgh Courier.

The other part of our history lesson was all about slavery and how the men were beaten and the women raped by the white master because the mistress always seemed to have a headache when the urge came. Though we learned much of that in school, the bulk of the story about slavery and its ravages was a part of family history-telling time. Just like the griot in Africa passed on their history to the young, so did our parents and grandparents. We kids all wanted to hear about the color of our skin and the mixture of our blood and why we had "funny colored" eyes – and so many other questions of why we were considered different from some others. We also wanted to know why there were so many colors of colored people – some black, some white and most all of those other colors in between. We wondered what difference it really made; after all, we all had to sit on the back of the bus and streetcar behind the colored sign and in the first car behind the engine on the train.

I remember so well, every time I look at one of the artifacts in my home, how I came upon that brown leather sign with only one word on it – Colored. My sister and I attended college at Tuskegee Institute, now Tuskegee University, in Alabama. We traveled to and from school by train. The first times we traveled together, we sat in the colored coach with other students. Eventually, however, we realized that we could better our lot by speaking Spanish and wearing our military-looking school uniforms on our train trips. When we first boarded the train in Cheehaw, Alabama with the other students, we had to comply with the colored rules since all of the other students knew "what" we were. On our first change of trains, however, we went into our first attempt at subterfuge – we "passed" for something other than Colored.

When the train stopped at its many water-loading places, my sister and I stayed on the train and did very little moving about. Nevertheless, we think because of our uniforms and since we were sitting in the proper coach, the Red Cross volunteers would come up to the train and offer us donuts and coffee and soft drinks – which we readily accepted and for which we were truly grateful. It was after the first successful sojourn as something other than coloreds that I promised myself to get one of those COLORED signs and keep it, just in case. The in case rarely came up – and for that we were again truly grateful.

My sister and I learned a very valuable lesson from the "passing" experience. We learned that we did not have to be oppressed by ignorance or conform to the social expectations of our day. We knew that we could play sports or cook dinner or repair a tire or prime a carbuerator or even wield a soldering iron or welding rod. We could be the leader as well as the follower.

My siblings and I were well-informed about those things that women were expected to do – wash and iron the clothes, wash dishes. We also were taught what men were bound to do – empty the trash, cut and bring the wood and light the fire. Mainly, however, we were assured that each of us were independent individuals, each responsible for our own lives. We learned, thank God, how to live in a man's world.

THE WAILING WALL

The Wailing Wall

    Wall of Fire

        Fiery Furnace

            On the Surface

                In the Forest – Punji Stakes

Mac never made it back to Camp Alpha. It took nine and a half months to identify his remains. They could have asked his mother.

But—

It's just as bad for my friend Lily. Lily was a nurse back in Nam. Mac's mom lost her only child. But – Lily stood by and watched so many die. She doesn't feel guilty for having stood by and seen those last gasps for air. Lily doesn't regret having lied to Mac and so many others when she told them that everything would be okay.

Lily actually got used to amputating limbs, binding up the stubs and rolling the gurney back to the ward and even shedding a few tears because the patient was still alive.

But a few months ago, Lily got back to the States and started work at an inner-city hospital. She had watched so many soldiers die in the Nam and had nursed even many more back to health.

But now – now they won't even let her hang an IV without permission. Lily learned how to go through blood and mud. She learned how to push aside guts to get to the fragments.

And sometimes, like me, Lily cries. By the way, Lily isn't a nurse anymore. And neither is Maureen. Linda quit. So did Rose.

Do you America wonder why?

Well, you should know. After all, you signed the Quit Deed.

HELP!!

Little girl – war!
All she knew was the word Help…
Didn't know what help
She wanted cause she couldn't explain what
Help she needed.
So the medic came and asked
"What's the matter?"
All she could say was "I don't know"

I FORGOT

The longer I wait for the reunion conference, the more I remember just how much I forgot.

I FORGOT because of my road-blocked brain. My Vietnam-time brain-road had so many stopovers.

I FORGOT the reason I went to Vietnam.

I FORGOT, for just a moment, to thank God for my safe return from that combat zone.

I FORGOT how I actually enjoyed working from sunup to sundown. Sometimes working for 18 to 22 hours a day was so rewarding.

I FORGOT how much it mattered whether a Viet Cong soldier was killed or whether it was an American soldier who lost his battle. All dead people are dead.

I FORGOT how many of my acquaintances and a few of my friends left me at the "office" never to return. Some were caught in ambush. Some were wounded by sniper fire. A 122mm rocket blew up the hootch of my guys. Some were wounded and never returned to my road-blocked brain. My Vietnam-time brain-road had so many stopovers.

I FORGOT how many times I went to the bunker: it was supposed to get me out of harm's way.

I FORGOT the time the CO had to come to my room, shake me awake, and remind me that whenever the incoming alarm sounded, I was to go to the bunker. (I remember that I remembered to take my cigarettes and bottle even though I forgot my flak jacket) I even forgot who brought me that fifth of Crown Royal every day!

I FORGOT so much. I've even forgotten what I forgot
But, wonder of wonders! I never forgot my friends. I know that
those friendships were forged in the heat of battle.

I never forgot Grendel and Joanne and Mickey and Effie and Marion
C and Betty B and Mary Jo and Betty T. I never forgot the Shirleys,
the Marys, the Joanies, the Donnas, the Claires, the Pats, the Annas
nor the Lauras. They are forever here in my heart...They help me
through the nightmares and PTSD. And the very moment that I
recognize a bad period approaching, I call on my Vietnam sisters who
helped me through my Vietnam-time and at least one or two of you
were always at one of those stopovers on my Vietnam-time road.

And now, I get a chance to offer my sincere thanks to all of my
sisters. Thanks for listening when I tried to be "mama" and thanks
for ignoring me when you thought it best. Thanks for inviting me to
enjoy a swim with you in our little backyard pool. Thanks for being
my friend. Thanks for being my friend! May God bless you all.

JUST FACES!

We're more than just faces

Like models in a magazine

No one cares who they are

And though labels can be the blindfolds

Of our lives, we can't, we shan't

Continue as nameless faces

What's worse? A nameless face

A faceless name

My heart cries out – I am more than just

A face

I'm more than just a name

Titles be damned but let the world know

That

I am more than just a face

I live, I breathe, I'm totally me

No matter what you think you see

My name is legend just in case

But I'm much more than just a face

ANGUISH

All you Jesse Jacksons

    Benjamin Hooks

    Parren Mitchells

    Yes, even Coretta Scott Kings

    When is the last time you went to a movie? Went with the little folks – no not just little folks – that's not what I mean – but when is the last time you went into a movie house when a "Black" movie was on – on an Army Base – when the only white folks at the flick were the five managers – four were on special hire tonight –after all, "Black" Flick – and the white folks behind the counter selling dry ass popcorn (soggy?) – and chocolate shit that melts in your hand – not in your mouth.

    I've gone lots of times – it just really sunk in tonight though – we want so much to laugh – we want so much to be happy – to be involved – to share happiness and a smile.

    We're supposed to laugh when we go to a Richard Pryor movie – and we try – even when it's not funny – like when the little white girl wanted straight teeth so badly – her folks couldn't afford to get braces so the little girl made braces of her own –out of plain old wire she found in the alley behind the corner grocery store. When her dad saw her, he could only mutter, "Oh my God," as he fought back the anguish and tears.

But when we first saw the little girl's predicament, we laughed.

I wrote this in 1972 or 1973. Is it finished?

July 2010 – That was over forty years ago. As I read today, I want so much to believe that everything has changed. I would be deceiving myself though. Now it's not only the Black folks that laugh – it's the whites and the Latinos and the Arabs and the Asians. The difference now though is that all of us are frustrated. All of us are crying as we look at today's flicks. No musicals at the movies – but "America's Got Talent" and "American Idol" fools us into believing everything is hunky dory, as our grandparents used to say.

Another difference now – I didn't have PTSD back in '71 or '72. I can't look at those so-called patriotic movies. I can't even watch cable TV with all the violence. Everything is violence. Those reality I-Box-type games have adults playing gang killer against their own children. Back in the day, at least the little children only used wooden guns to "shoot" as they played Cowboys and Indians. I can't go to the concert for fear somebody will throw a firecracker in celebration of the noise – the rockets red glare – the bombs bursting in air. Helicopters still scare me.

"Why are you laughing, Lucki?" they ask me. My reply, "I'm laughing just to keep from crying." Will this feeling of helplessness ever go away? I'm still stuck in Vietnam. I still feel helpless. Will it ever go away or will I just laugh myself to sleep? Laugh myself to sleep! Laugh myself to sleep!

I WAS CONVINCED I WAS RIGHT

AND THEY DIDN'T KNOW ENOUGH ABOUT IT TO EVEN HAVE AN OPINION.

A silly millisecond later, I found out just how much I didn't know. The ammo dump was blowing and my head was still on my shoulders as I looked out the door of my hootch. Wow, this was the big one and I wanted to really see what it looked like. After all, I was less than four city blocks from the MELEE and wasn't 'gonna hide' from the big bang. I hadn't been in country long enough or even in a hot spot of imminent danger to realize the gravity of the situation.

It was a little longer than a millisecond but when the blast/shock actually hit my position, I was so unprepared. The next thing I knew, I was pulling myself out from beneath my bunk, brushing my shocked self off and recalling that I had been schooled. Through my training as a Nuclear, Biological and Chemical Warfare (NBC) specialist, I had studied enough about delivery systems and effects of blast and knew of the delay factor. In my intelligence training, I had been well schooled as an interrogator of prisoners of war. I knew the delay was often more dangerous than the IMPACT. There was an inherent danger in looking at a blast—when the shock wave got to you, it was basically (evolutionally) much too late to draw my head out of harm's way.

That seemed to be the herald—My entire three years in Vietnam were fraught with danger. I knew it but found that the brushing off after the impact was what kept me seeking and searching. I wanted to learn enough to eventually master my job. If I couldn't get to "Charlie" I would at least know I had been in his house against all odds—woman in a combat zone, etc, etc.

THE KISS AT THE TOP OF THE HILL

I DIDN'T LIKE BOB HOPE-EVEN THEN-STILL DON'T. But even now I remember like it was just last week.
My roommate was in charge of 1st LOG PIO in Vietnam. So I always knew ahead of time when somebody big was coming to perform even though it took some real heavy maneuvering on my part.

Fact is, I had all kinds of Top Secret and special intelligence security clearances but one of the best kept secrets in all of Vietnam was the EXACT TIME that the big names were coming to entertain the troops. Hell, I even knew when McNamara was coming in to get some new information for his diary. Of course I didn't realize that he was engineering the damn war so he could write a million dollar best seller 30 years later. I knew all about the secret incursions into Laos and Cambodia. Every time a big American or allied military operation was to take place I knew about it. I was privy to information on damned near every air sortie north of the DMZ before the planes took off.

Shit, between all the information to which I was officially privy and all the intelligence I generated through my own prowess as an analyst, I was the smartest, most intelligent and most informed soldier in all of Vietnam.

Wrong! Don't believe it! With all of that stuff I knew, my roommate was my hero. I put her on a pedestal and made promises that even I knew I would have trouble fulfilling and maybe couldn't even keep.

I promised one time that I would get filet mignon for supper that day. I did! Once I promised a new battery for her CJ-5 even though I knew that they were an almost non-existent commodity at that time. She got it though. Keep in mind that I wanted something from her too. So, I had no problem with the Vung Tau trip I promised. That next week-end, my buddy brought his LOH in and flew us out to the Coral Sea which was anchored down in the bay right out from Vung Tau. We had lunch at the Captain's table then mingled and danced with the crew until the Red Catcher Huey picked us up and snuck us back onto the 1st Av Bde chopper pad at Long Binh.

Yes, I made all of those promises so I'd be one of the first to know that a big name was coming in to entertain the troops and exactly when. You see, some of the troops from the field were usually on stand-down, or perhaps they were at Camp Alpha for DEROS or maybe just arriving in-country and waiting at the 90th Repl Depot. Many of them were patients at Long Binh's 24th Evac Hospital and even some came from the 3d Fld Hospital at Saigon. Too, there were zillions - or so it seemed - of support troops from Long Binh and Bien Hoa and those hot shots from Red Catcher (199th LIB).

Frankly, I wanted to know the exact date and time of the BIG Entertainment because I wanted a seat on the center aisle in the front row. Fortunately, my roommate came through and that particular Christmas morning at 0900, I was sitting in my proper place before the other troops were flown, bussed, trucked or jeeped in for the Bob Hope Show.

After the 2-hour show was over, I still had most of my creases in my fatigues. You see, the temperature in the Long Binh Amphitheater was sort of mild. It was only 92 degrees most of the day, but that hot sun beaming down was enough to melt a Tom & Jerry cup of ice cream and make a fish ask for a cool drink of water. It certainly wilted the troops.

That day was no different for me though - uniform-wise, that is. I had kept my buns right on the edge of the seat and my legs straight out in front.

At any rate, I was still pretty neat after the show and as I started walking up the steps to the top rim of the amphitheater I couldn't help but notice the faces of the troops. Some sad that it was over—some happy they had been able to stand down—some happy they had been able to see the Bob Hope Show—some tired from sitting so long in the hot sun. And then there was me. I had so many mixed emotions as I walked up that long hill.

But it all came together all of a sudden. All my sadness and happiness—all my promises paid off. There at the top of the hill stood a young man—among many others. But this young man—no more than 18 years of age, caught me from a long way off. He probably didn't know that he drew me like a giant magnet. Strictly not my type as I now think about it—but such magnetism.

Yet, I walked up to that young, filthy, sweaty, sloppy soldier standing there, so forlorn with a look of hopelessness and despair and dejection as his beacon. I guess God must have led me to him. I walked up to him, wished him a merry Christmas and a happy New Year, grabbed him and put one big kiss on this youngster at the top of the hill.

He threw down his M-16 and with all eyes still on us he yelled to the world--"I don't need nothing else! I don't need no gun!" His happiness was there for all to see.

And as he practically swooned, all I could think of was I didn't like Bob Hope. I STILL DON'T.

MATTER OF RESPECT

All I said was, "General, your fly is open." After flashing me an undercover grin he thanked me, zipped up his pants and kept on to where he was headed. Somebody should have alerted him by now but all I heard was several negative comments. "Oh well," I thought, "Everybody can't be appreciative." I liked the general. In fact, I was a bit embarrassed that the General had probably walked down several corridors with his fly open and none of the men had the nerve, grit, gall nor audacity to tell him about it. Nevertheless, that incident didn't help my credibility.

I don't think the men really knew what to think—they certainly tried categorizing me. Their opinions certainly got skewed, I was sure, when they saw my violent reaction to a moment of disrespect there in the AOC one day. All they heard was this loud thud. Everybody started laughing at how silly "Red" looked sprawled out on the deck. "Red" was a young new guy who had made a very unwise decision to "touch" me inappropriately. I realize he might have been tempted by my stance—I was leaning over my desk doing some map coordinates for my daily intelligence update. But "Red" made the mistake of patting me on my buns—that insult to me and my body caused me to react -violently I think.

As soon as "Red" touched me, I came up with a right handed, back hand smash that sent him reeling over one desk, into another and onto the floor. As he was attempting to pick himself up he had the nerve to ask me, "What did you do that for?" I was naturally livid with rage and my answer made him know that if he ever touched me again it would be his last moment on earth. My sidearm, a .45, was laying on the left side of my desk and only by the grace of God did I not pick it up and blow "Red" to kingdom come.

It was all about respect – if I respected me I most assuredly would not brook disrespect from others. One hint of self-disrespect I knew would only open the floodgate–it always had.

One of the major pieces of wisdom I always wanted to pass on to the new women arrivals into country had to do with standing clean and tall in their uniform, doing their jobs in the most efficient manner possible and above all taking pride in themselves. Some of the younger women seemed to feel that their presence among so many men gave them the right to treat some of those men with disrespect in terms of snubbing many of them. There were 300 men to every one woman on Long Binh. I was able to get across the fact that many of the men were hungry for companionship of any kind with women from home whom they called "round-eyes"—some hadn't even laid an eye on an American woman since arriving on Vietnam. Both the women and men knew that Vietnam was no place for "hanky-panky" though several met life-companions while there.

> I had to remind some of the youngsters that though life was full of "handsome" choices there at Long Binh their behavior might keep them from making friends – and they certainly wouldn't have that many choices when they got back to the states. It was that old adage all in

place - "be nice to people on the way up – you never know who you might meet on the way down."

When I first arrived at Long Binh in 1967 I wasn't surprised to see hootches designated for the men to have legalized sex with Vietnamese prostitutes. The hootches were approved and the prostitutes were examined and certified to be sexually healthy before they were allowed to work on the military base. I was convinced, for some albeit archaic reason, that men who were in a combat zone had to satisfy their testosteronically-dictated urges for sexual gratification – or they wouldn't be able to work. That strategy seemed to work during the Korean War.

About six months later I learned that the prostitutes were no longer legal on Long Binh and the designated hootches were to be closed. I was an active advocate of those "whore houses" only because I felt it was a safe way for men to satisfy their feral urges even while practicing "safe" sex. Safe at that time meant that since the prostitutes were "healthy" in the legal military sense that the men would experience fewer, if any, sexually transmitted diseases. I was informed later that the reason for the closure was occasioned by anger from military wives in the states who felt Uncle Sam was advocating adulterous and promiscuous sexual behavior by their husbands and mates.

Out of my league – but I really thought it was a brilliant maneuver. It was no accident then that the STD rate rose exponentially. It was certainly worse when the unrequited urges of the "boss" led on many occasions to his harsh manners as some poor soul got chewed out just for being.

It was really hard not to have compassion for

those troops – it was hard that I could not help them find a way. But then, I guess everything turned out – I never heard of a guy expiring for lack of sex.

    I do know from experience however that adrenalin is its own "Master."

NOTHING MORE TO PROVE

Nothing more to prove tells me that "the proof is (already) in the pudding." Ask yourself these questions – Did I do my best? When the job is done, did I do a good job or was it done just to "prove" that I could?

As we can live only in the present, we cannot predict what the next beholder will do or say. But then ask yourself, "Now that I have done this to the best of my ability, did I do it well? What more is there?"

I see those who served after us as well as younger heroines of today and I am so pleased that they are confirming their worth – yes, they do us proud – it says that we likely left a worthy legacy.

I often receive many compliments on my job well done. I thank all, but the final beholder has already received my efforts and confirmed their worth – I can truthfully and honorably accept with grace that we women in military service to this country, have

Nothing More to Prove

ONLY WHEN YOU DIE

Only when you die is your life complete. It is finished. Yet, only when you die do others ponder about your worth. We talk to the dead. We tell them how very much they were loved. We recount the joys we shared. We tell others how well you knew the dearly departed and how you were closer than a sister, a mother, a father or a brother. We look upon their contenance and proclaim how they look as if they were just sleeping.

My friends, we waste our own breath talking to the dead. Talk, my friends, to the living. Tell me how to be a better friend. Tell me where to take my laundry to get it cleaner. Tell me how to get better grades in the school of life. Help me glide to my "what's next" on a path that you helped to make smooth with your loving impact. Be my guide if you know the way. Walk beside me in faith knowing that God is in control.

Life for me depends on my keeping to the Golden Rule to "do unto others as you would have others do unto you." So, even though we know that without life we are nothing, we must accept the fact that only when you die is your life complete.

Rest in peace.

DID YOU? I'M JUST ASKING

Just tell me the truth, Doc. Did you do it on purpose? Or did you just didn't know any better? Or did you really mean to cripple me? I'm just asking! I'd really rather look at the bright side; but did you do it on purpose?

Is it my fault that I walk this way? Yes, one leg is shorter than the other, but they were both the same before the operation. Just tell me the truth, Doc. Did you do it on purpose or did you just didn't know any better? I'm just asking.

By the way, both the Mommie and the Daddy were really healthy young folks. But the baby had what they called a birth defect. Now that didn't show up on the ultrasound shots. So tell me, Doc, did you do it on purpose or did you just didn't know any better? I'm just asking.

But all that is gone water and the rain drop is just part of the mud puddle. I guess no matter how or why it happened, I'll still walk funny and the pain won't just go away.

Only thing I know to do now is forgive you. And I'll just have to keep on with that unanswered question. I must seek closure in my daily prayers. I will ask God to cleanse my mind of any bitterness. I must ask God to let me be kind to others even though I might believe that others are/were unkind to me. And I know that God will answer my prayer. I believe that God sustains me even through my pain.

But Doc, tell me the truth. Did you do it on purpose? Or did you just didn't know any better? I'M JUST ASKING.

HALF-WRAPPED

One day we all played softball
I sprained my ankle and
We all insisted
I go to the hospital

The nurse worked feverishly to
Comfort me.

The chopper came in with five WIA
Blood splattered all over the Q-hut.

    STAT! STAT!

I'll never forget the love and caring
And unselfishness I saw in her eyes
As she kept on apologizing so many times for
Having to leave my ankle
Half-wrapped.

I helped with the emergency—but I wish
I could find that nurse just to say

Thank You!

YOU INSIDE MY BODY

Did you ever dream of finding a lot of money—ready to party? Then you wake up—nothing but a clenched fist,

After the confusion—

>23 March 1996
>Jacksonville, FL

After the confusion—I remember—

I've been so long looking for my body.

    Did I leave it in Vietnam or did I leave it at "The Wall?"

If it is here inside my life I wonder what sustains me?

    You there! No, I mean you here inside me, you, you, you make me cry. You make me dream of knives and soldiers—soldiers and knives. You've made me wield my sword to cut up whichever villain that you, yourself manufactured inside me. Thank God, the villain is never me. Funny though, the heroine is also never me.

    I step through mine fields in my dreams—I never die. I fire the M-60 which propels the deadly shells at the tank occupied by—by—I never can—I never do—will I ever?—identify the occupants.

    I've never been able to determine if my target is friend or foe. Yet I dream—superficial dreams—ugly dreams—bloody bodies on a battlefield—men or women—all soldiers—but I still never know whether it's friend or foe.

Daytimes, when the wonder of quiet envelopes me, I soar like an eagle and look over the greenery and beauty that God wrought. Soon, however, the wonderful quiet is shattered. The quiet, like the day, goes suddenly away. Just as night can never become day, nor day night, the quiet does not saunter away. The quiet is, simply put, no longer there. What replaces quiet might come as the sound of a shoe being dropped on a carpet or a cork being extracted from a bottle of champagne or a tire blowing out or the backfire of an automobile or even just the thought of the "rockets red glare" and "bombs bursting in air."

Then, all of a sudden, my life that is still in search of my body, cries out. Sometimes, I shake after the startling effect of the lightning-fast quiet gone. But most of the time my inner must adjust and calibrate and modulate the stress.

The counselor keeps telling me to "join a veteran's group, talk it out and it will all go away." Will it ever? Won't it ever? Want it ever?

I don't know! I don't know! I don't know!

JUST STOP

Just Stop!

    Make Love to the Water

Its flowing breath will touch the shores and leave an everlasting whiff of love--
Before you go leave a footprint in the sand.
And though the water will vanquish it, you, yes you, will know where once you trod.
You, who are here on the earth, will surely disappear just like the footprint.

You don't have to feel the power to know it's there. In your mind the power shrieks. It tells you when it's time. The carpet is not the swallower; neither can the turbine blow away the veil. But your mind, your mind can take the smallest pebble and see it as a mighty boulder. It is like lava just formed. But soon, like the lava, it might become like fallow ground.

But you, make love to the water. Leave a footprint in the sand.

Then, go gracefully through the door to meet your maker and know--

Know that you are free.

OH DANNY BOY

Danny wanted to make love to me
    I could see it in his eyes
But he couldn't even speak to me
    After several stuttering tries.

He finally took my hand
    And then he started to cry
I don't know how I knew just then
    This would be his last goodbye.

Danny tripped as he ran to the chopper
    But took time to look back and wave
I don't know how I knew just then
    Qui Nhon would be his grave

It was Larry who called and told me
    How Danny had smothered the grenade
And save the lives of the other three
    When they went out on that raid.

I've often wondered in these last few years
    If we'd had that moment of joy
Whether on another luckless battlefield
    I'd lose another Danny boy.

INCOMING

INCOMING!

    INCOMING!

        I must have awakened out of habit—for a moment.

But out of sheer exhaustion I could only think—"So what!"

    I don't know how much later but my C.O. was shaking me awake demanding I join the others in the bunker.

        God! I was tired! Funny though—on my way to the bunker I forgot my helmet and my Flak jacket—but not my bottle.

        My bottle—my alcohol. So unforgiving, my companion. It dulled my senses and let me feel like a warrior.

A stupid warrior!

    A stupid war!

        A stupid warrior in a stupid war!

I'll never forgive "them" for that.

    But just today—just today—I can forgive me

Forgive me
    Forgive me
        Forgive me!

SISTERS

I feel some better now

And one thing I do know

Sisters don't just up and leave

Unless they're called to go

My Sister used to tell us

When we were young back home

You just gotta keep on living

Cause all goodbyes ain't gone.

And I don't feel like celebrating

Cause my sister had to go

I just keep feeling selfish

And sometimes a little low.

But since she didn't belong to me

Cause she was God's alone

I can accept the fact

That my sister's just gone home!

And I feel some better now

Cause there's one thing I do know

Sisters just don't up and leave

Unless they're called to go.

NO PURPLE HEART

No Purple Heart!

    Didn't get shot!

        Brain got wounded!

            Can't put a cast on it!

Didn't know where the pain came from. That's when I found that they didn't know either. Asked myself, "What's wrong with me?" Couldn't for the life of me stop those scary dreams, those nightmares that so often consumed and ruled and ruined my efforts to rest.

    Just talk it out. That's what they said. Mostly, men at the meeting. Found out some lying was going on. Figured out why. Even though many of the symptoms were valid, the explanations of the source seemed sort of skewed. Aha! Just recalled that testostoronic machinations demand: little fish on hook—big fish story.

    But even though no purple heart, didn't get shot, the PTSD is still bane and wrecking so many.

No valor!

    No purple heart!

        But I hurt too!

            But I hurt too!

ABOUT THE AUTHOR

Doris I "Lucki" Allen has had a long and successful career in the fields of organizational development and interpersonal communications. The highly decorated former military intelligence officer received numerous awards and was inducted into the United States Military Intelligence Corps Hall of Fame in June, 2009. Her awards include a Bronze Star with Two Oak Leaf Clusters, the United Nations Service Medal and the Vietnam Cross of Gallantry among others. She served three tours in Vietnam during that major conflict. Dr. Allen served throughout the United States, Southeast Asia, Japan and Europe and retired from the US Army in 1980 after serving 30 years.

Dr. Allen is a graduate of Tuskegee University (Institute), BS Physical Education: Ball State University; MA Psychological Counseling; and The Wright Institute; Ph.D. Psychology & Organizational Development.

The Congressional Black Caucus, the United Church of Christ and the City of San Francisco have honored Dr. Allen. She has also been honored by the Cultural Society of Chesapeake, VA and is part of the permanent exhibit of the Vietnam War Years at the President Lyndon Baines Johnson Museum in Austin, Texas and the ACES Museum in Philadelphia, PA.

At present and for the past 30 years Dr. Allen has been delving into the field of social psychology. "I have become increasingly aware of the ever-present subtlety of mass media and its deleterious causation of man's inhumanity to man" she says. Her "ministry" is to give back to the world whatever the world gave to her with the most attention to those who have not or won't (sic). She is a mentor and works with persons who are striving for intellectual excellence through academic achievement. She also works with persons affected with HIV/AIDS in both the United States, Mexico and several nations in Africa.

Retired Chief Warrant Officer Allen is a Life-Member of NABMW (National Association of Black Military Women, Life-member of VVA (Vietnam Veterans of America), Life-member of DAV (Disabled American Veterans) Life-member of VFW (Veterans of Foreign Wars) and Life-member of Vietnam Veterans of Diablo Valley (California) She is a charter member of WIMSA (Women In Military Service for America). She is a life-long member of Heroines of Jericho (Prince Hall Masons) and Daughter Elks (IBPOEofW).

Her other military decorations include Bronze Star Medal w/2 Oak Leaf Clusters; Meritorious Service Award; Army Commendation Medal; Good Conduct Medal (6th Award); Army Occupation Medal (Japan); National Defense Service Medal; Korean Service Medal; Vietnam Service Medal (10 Campaigns); Vietnam Cross of Gallantry w/Palm; United Nations Service Medal; Republic of Vietnam Campaign Medal; Presidential Unit Commendation; and Meritorious Unit Commendation.

Made in the USA
San Bernardino, CA
19 November 2014